Of Poverty and Wealth

The 21st Century

Julian Ashbourn

Copyright © 2017 Julian Ashbourn
All Rights Reserved
ISBN: 1542857457
ISBN -13: 978-1542857451

This book is dedicated to my dear wife Joanna, who understands the distinction between poverty and wealth in the real sense, more keenly than anyone I know. Without the wealth of her unending support I would undoubtedly have been a poorer man.

Contents

1	Introduction	Pg 1
2	Two Sides of a Coin	Pg 7
3	Heritage	Pg 17
4	Character	Pg 27
5	National Situations	Pg 33
6	Industry	Pg 41
7	Accumulation	Pg 51
8	Education	Pg 59
9	Appreciation	Pg 67
10	Creativity	Pg 75
11	Understanding	Pg 81
12	Morality	Pg 91
13	Generosity	Pg 99
14	Meanness	Pg 107
15	Nature	Pg 113
16	Conclusion	Pg 119
17	Epilogue	Pg 127

1. Introduction

We live in the 21st century where humanity has come a long way from its early beginnings as hunters and gatherers in harmony with the natural world. Whereas we were once just another animal among animals we have, through what we often describe as our superior intelligence, come to dominate the world around us and all its natural creations. This formidable power has also bred a certain attitude, or state of mind, which seems equally divorced from our animate neighbours with whom we share this Earth. As a consequence, our values seem to have become somewhat distorted; increasingly so perhaps with every generation.

In particular, our view of what constitutes wealth and poverty and how we prioritise the importance of the same has become rather odd, if not bordering on the bizarre. We have become obsessed by celebrity and material wealth, placing these above all else in our estimation and understanding. Younger generations are brainwashed from birth to think likewise and to pursue a life of material gain. Many in the public eye state freely that the only thing that is important in life is making money. Those who are most successful in this context are placed on a pedestal and worshipped accordingly, even to the extent of receiving public honours for doing nothing but becoming rich. It seems that those who spend their time on Earth in abject selfishness are rewarded accordingly and held in the highest esteem.

Not to make money is aligned with failure in life and those who fall into this category tend to be despised or pitied and are invariably shunned. Those who give unselfishly of their time in helping others, with no expectation of recognition or reward, we mostly never hear about. Fortunately, they do exist and walk among us like angels amid the hoards of ordinary people with all their problems, trials and tribulations.

Between these extremes we have, among other things, the phoney charities that, actually, are not charities at all but exist as businesses for the benefit

Introduction

of the executive officers who pay themselves obscenely large salaries while others collect on their behalf. These institutions exist to assuage the public conscience and give the impression that we are a caring society. Those charities that focus upon foreign aid are particularly suspect, with much of their wealth never getting anywhere near the regions that they are ostensibly collecting for. However, these institutions are again praised with their crooked directors often receiving public honours accordingly. Meanwhile, the poor and needy remain poor and needy.

The large multi-national corporations that become super rich, do so by systematically cheating their customers, whether they be business or private clients. The giant IT corporations are a very good example of this and one does not have to look very far to see instances of gross corruption, unfair business practices and the creation of monopolies. They are often aided and abetted by politicians with the line between commerce and politics becoming increasingly blurred. This is perhaps unsurprising as politics has long since ceased as a mechanism for managing the affairs of countries and has become a self serving global institution with individual politicians observing but one goal; to make as much money for themselves as they possibly can when in office, while simultaneously forging and developing the web of contacts necessary to continue the practice when no longer in office.

All of this in pursuit of wealth. Wealth beyond the needs of any individual, but still it remains the single goal of life for such individuals. The more accumulated, the more greedy they become. We have created a global society based upon the acquisition of wealth for its own sake. A universal culture of greed.

The irony is that this attitude and focus aligns wealth purely with money and material gain. This is what people are taught by example right from the start and it is only the exceptional that learn to reason for themselves and see beyond the shallowness of this dreadful greed culture. Those few that do will understand that true wealth exists only in the heart and soul, and has absolutely nothing to do with material wellbeing. It is nurtured by kindness and compassion towards all life and burnished by experience and understanding. Those plastic politicians and celebrities know nothing of

Introduction

such things and waste their lives wallowing in pointless materialism. And yet, like everyone else, they leave this world with nothing more than they possessed when they entered it. In fact, their lives are completely worthless as they, throughout all their precious time on Earth, contribute nothing to the common good of understanding.

Those who are able to reason, to understand and to show compassion towards others, including animals, enrich the human condition by further developing this understanding for the common good. Indeed, they are the wealthy for they are wealthy in spirit and that is a wealth that is never diminished.

I am now desperately ill and I don't know whether I shall have the time to finish this book or, if I do, whether it will ever be published, let alone read by anyone. Nevertheless, I am filled with a conviction that there remain words that should be articulated in print. That, in our dumbed down, politically correct, shallow society, there are things that should not be left unsaid. The Great Deception can surely not endure forever. Someone needs to sow a seed of realisation. A seed which may be carefully nurtured and cultivated until a crop ensues, upon which others may feed and become stronger in their own conviction as to the true meaning of poverty and wealth, and how to fashion their lives around this realisation. Further, to impart this understanding to their children, that they might also be able to distinguish between what is true and wholesome and what is shallow and meaningless in this context. Maybe, for some people at least, this book will be the seed. I certainly hope so.

2. Two Sides of a Coin

A coin has two sides with opposing designs upon each and yet, it is a single object which one appreciates as such. And so it is with many things in life. Positive and negative, light and dark, north and south and other factors which may be perceived as opposites are nonetheless related and often more closely than may at first be appreciated. In Chinese philosophy the concept of Yin and Yang describes these relationships. Originally conceived as the light and dark sides of a slope, Yin and Yang have developed into a higher significance that relates to all things in life. While ostensibly opposites, each contains a little of the other and both exist simultaneously within all aspects of life. Indeed, Yin and Yang reflect the patterns and relationships that exist within the natural world. It is a world of harmonies, contrasts, but especially relationships. Everything is related to everything else in one sense or another within a complex web of dependencies. This is how the natural world evolves and prospers. Nothing really exists in isolation. Neither do states. An object or condition may only be described in relation to another. We know something is hot because it is not cold. We appreciate light because it is not dark. Hard is not soft. North is not south. Order is not chaos. We use one to describe the other, but they are nonetheless related.

At some point, as we move between one state and the opposite state, the two become blurred and we are at a natural juncture from where we could progress in either direction. If we look at the face of a coin, we identify one side. If we turn it over, we identify the opposite side. But what if we look at the coin edgewise on? We see neither side, until we tilt it a little, one way or the other. In fact, the two opposites are very closely related and are, in fact, inseparable. An increase in one resulting in a decrease of the other, with the sum remaining the same within a harmonious whole, within which opposites often attract. They may be even more closely related depending upon our definitions of the two states. In one sense, it may not even matter which state receives our focus, as they are so closely related, the distinction between them being often perceptual rather than real.

The reader might well question what all this has to do with poverty and wealth. Much has to do with our definition of poverty and wealth within this particular duality. Certainly, they are two sides of a particular coin, but which coin? In our modern world we have come to equate wealth purely in monetary terms. We evaluate everything either as to what it costs, what it is worth or how much profit we can wring from it. We believe that anything which is of great cost must be truly valuable, whilst that which is of low cost, or no cost, must be worthless. Furthermore, we have come to regard the acquisition of money as an indicator of success in life. Therefore, those who have made money and have surrounded themselves with material goods must be wealthy. Those who have little money and few material possessions must be poor. Our entire global society is aligned with this point of view and, because we relate money with success, we teach our children that the only goal that is worthwhile is to make money. We confirm this assertion by placing the rich on a pedestal and regarding them as icons to be envied and copied. In true Yin and Yang manner, we therefore condemn the poor to be despised as lower class citizens.

We may observe this behaviour anywhere where human beings gather together. Even in social meetings, often the first question asked, when meeting someone for the first time, is what one does for a living. The answer produces, in the mind of the questioner, an immediate image of financial worth. If one is a stockbroker or politician, the answer will bring forth approval. If the same person were to answer that he is a milkman or perhaps unemployed, the conversation will probably come to a premature conclusion as he will be considered as not worth speaking to. If someone is asked in which area they live, their answer will similarly produce a defined level of interest according to the questioners perception of the area. Mayfair or Kensington will elicit a different response than Luton or Upminster.

One could provide many more such examples of how we judge everything in material terms. The worst of it is that, not only do we judge the worth of the individual in these terms, but we will actively curtail or enhance the opportunities open to them based upon this artificial metric. Indeed, we maintain an effective class system based upon material wellbeing and the perceived standing of the individual within this materialistic society. The barriers established by these classes often prove difficult, if not impossible to cross. Other factors, such as appearance and accent for example, are also indicators which immediately categorise the individual, based upon their association with material wealth. We assume that the wealthy will speak with a particular accent and dress in a particular manner. Similarly the materially poor will have their own distinctive appearance and accent which will characterise them immediately. The story of Professor Higgins in the play Pygmalion, by George Bernard Shaw, took a whimsical view of being able to place individuals geographically and socially by their accent and, conversely, being able to establish an individual, in this case Eliza Doolittle, in an altogether different class by changing both their accent and appearance. Although a work of fictional entertainment, Pygmalion reflected much about our materialistic society and the assumptions we make within it. Again, there is a Yin and Yang aspect of this particular scenario, proving how closely the two opposites are actually related. In this case, they were bridged by a common denominator in the form of Eliza Doolittle.

So far, the distinctions of wealth in a material sense have been stressed. But this is surely wealth in its most shallow and meaningless incarnation. One might well argue that it is much better to be wealthy in terms of knowledge and understanding. The individual that accrues true knowledge and understanding is wealthy regardless of societal position or acknowledgement. The individual who adds to this the wealth of compassion and kindness is truly wealthy in any society. The opposite of this wealth of knowledge is of course ignorance. The opposite of compassion and kindness being intolerance and cruelty. They are often of the same coin whose other face is material wealth and they can be closer fellows than one might imagine.

As a result of this closeness, we must be careful with our definitions. Why do we only consider those who have accrued money as wealthy? Why not those who have accrued knowledge? Or those who have accrued humanity? Often, the man who is materially rich and placed on a pedestal may be destitute in terms of true knowledge and understanding or, especially, humanity. This may particularly be the case for those who have inherited material wealth and position. Such attributes often encourage an arrogance and intolerance in equal measure, with those in such a position looking down upon others and treating them with contempt. And yet, some of those treated with contempt may, in terms of knowledge and understanding, be infinitely more wealthy, as might those with an abundance of compassion and kindness towards all living things.

All history has shown us that the darker sides of humanity and its trajectory into modern times, have very often been characterised and orchestrated by such distinctions. Greed, and a sense of superiority associated with material worth, have so often pitched brother against brother and nation against nation, sometimes in the most cruel and horrifying manner. And yet, still we persist in this adoration of material wealth above all else. Those who acquire it continue to believe that they are better, in all respects, than those who do not. They strut about and pose in all their aggressive arrogance, without realising the futility of such a shallow perspective.

Of course, not everyone who is wealthy behaves in such a manner. Some are sensitive to the human condition and therefore more altruistic in their attitude. Similarly, those who are materially poor may equally be aggressive and arrogant. There are exceptions to every rule.

It is a complex situation wherein opposites and even extremes may be closely related, the one readily tipping into the other at a certain point, depending upon a particular perspective or situation. It is further complicated by the absurd association of monetary worth with success which has become a hallmark of global society. Everything we see, hear or do is tainted with this association. The more we focus upon such shallowness, the less attention we pay towards wealth of other kinds. We may witness this in the deterioration of education, excepting of course in subjects associated with making money. Appreciation of other, more cerebral factors being dismissed as irrelevant. However, as a consequence of the complex relationships and dependencies that exist in all life, we adopt such attitudes at our peril. In particular, they represent the slippery slope of deception which, once embarked upon, is very difficult to leave. Those on this slope try to convince others that this is the way things should be, in order to justify their own position. But we must not listen to such assertions, lest we become tainted ourselves.

3. Heritage

We often think of heritage in terms of the celebration of culture and history. We like to preserve historic 'heritage' sites of special interest and we celebrate culture in terms of literature and the arts in general, but also the prevailing attitude and characteristics of human population. Many parts of the world are rich in heritage of this sort, although they can also squander their heritage via short sited government. A good example of this may be found in modern Britain, where the understanding of 500 years or more of distinguished history is being thrown away and even actively denied in some quarters, as the all pervading culture of greed takes over.

Heritage in this sense is not something which is created over night but is a product of people who had a national pride and the desire to create and move things forward at their particular time. Very often, this national spirit was accompanied by a mixture of courage, compassion and ingenuity which created the artifacts that we now celebrate as heritage. Consequently, there may be a wealth or poverty of heritage, depending upon the country or regime in question.

But there is another way of looking at heritage and that is in terms of inheritance, both national and personal. There may be a perceived wealth or poverty of inheritance, according to time, place and perspective. At a personal level, one may inherit wealth, power and position through no activity or expertise of our own. Similarly, one may inherit poverty through no fault of our own. This somewhat cruel accident of birth has caused many divisions throughout history with the privileged classes looking down upon the poor as almost another species, one to be exploited but rarely helped. Of course, there have been exceptions to this general rule but, nevertheless, such class distinctions have caused many bitter confrontations, uprisings and, occasionally revolutions. Even today, a strong class system exists and prevails in many countries and, for those born into the poorer class, life can be very difficult due to this simple accident of birth. For those born into a more prosperous class, they often believe that it is their right to be born into such a life of privilege and do everything they can to maintain such a distinction, especially if it is to their benefit. Furthermore, they will often maintain this distinction by force, as we have seen so often throughout the history of our world.

However, at a personal level, much depends upon our definition of poverty and wealth. One may have all the riches imaginable and yet remain morally destitute and lacking in understanding of all kinds. Material wealth is shallow and, once experienced, quickly becomes meaningless. Many therefore cling to it, almost in desperation, as they cannot imagine what their life would mean without it. This is understandable as, for many, their life would indeed be meaningless and is, in fact, meaningless with or without wealth. Indeed, wealth is only meaningful if it is used positively for the wellbeing and happiness of others. For those who just sit upon their vast wealth and consume for their own pleasure, both their wealth and their lives will reflect the meanness and shallowness of this position.

There are, as always, exceptions to the rule, but even these exceptions may not be what they seem. For the wealthy to perform 'charitable services' such as appearing in the media to encourage others to donate to some charity or another while they themselves donate nothing, simply reflects an arrogance and ego based upon selfishness. Even those who may contribute a small amount to some named charity, of which they know nothing, and do so publicly, this is not generally helpful. If, on the other hand, they gave their time and kindness to help alleviate the suffering and misery of others, then this would indeed be meaningful, especially if they used their wealth to facilitate this upon a grand scale. The super rich rarely see things this way, especially if their wealth and position is inherited.

Conversely, the poorer classes have often generated exceptional individuals who have given generously of their time and expertise in order to make the world a better place. Even from a scientific perspective, this has often been the case, with many individuals from poorer backgrounds going on to make important scientific discoveries or to work on subsequently important inventions for the common good. Similarly, in the arts, individuals have often come from undistinguished backgrounds to create wonderful works in both visual arts, literature and music. Even the greatest of all, such as Beethoven or Van Gogh, were rarely from the privileged classes. One could give many hundreds of similar examples.

An example of the principle is St Francis of Assisi and his followers who understood that, actually, you need no possessions at all in order to lead a good and meaningful life which, in his case, has benefited the lives of millions of others and continues to do so today. How many of today's super rich can claim the same? St Francis also showed that you may appreciate and draw strength from the natural world and all its wonders regardless of your particular position. This is a lesson that might usefully be propagated among the world's poor, in all nations, today.

Irrespective of material wealth and social standing, the poorer or less privileged classes may be enriched by the simple expedient of education. Good and comprehensive education is not difficult to provide and yet may transform the lives of millions of youngsters. We have understood this for many generations and yet, even in the most prosperous countries, there often remains a two-tier education system. One for the privileged classes and one for everybody else although, in some cases, no education at all. The respective governments could easily provide such an education and yet perceive it as in their interest to maintain this social division by ensuring that the masses remain either uneducated or poorly educated. Indeed, in some of the world's wealthiest countries, education has deteriorated markedly in recent years with good quality teaching becoming almost non-existent. How will such a system create a noble and meaningful heritage for the future? It will not.

So, we need to understand heritage in its purer sense, both personal and national. Heritage is neither a right nor an inevitability. We inherit the works of those who went before us, for better or for worse. The better works, we need to preserve and, perhaps more importantly, understand why we are preserving them and what their presence today really means. This is true of architecture, literature, the arts and culture. In all its forms, heritage may be celebrated and cared for. It may also be squandered and distorted. A well known castle in the English Midlands springs to mind which used to be a pleasure to visit. To quietly walk in its grounds, to admire the architecture and absorb the ambience of the authentic interiors, while also understanding its history and all those who have lived there. Now, it has been turned into a veritable theme park, with bouncy castles, so called 'attractions' and activities which have absolutely nothing to do with the castle and its history. This represents a tasteless, shameful betrayal of our heritage and does nothing to teach visitors of why the castle existed, its relationship to other English castles and its true place in history.

Why has this been done? Simply to make money. To ensure that the owners of the property squeeze as much money as possible out of this once noble building. To them, clearly, money is more important than heritage. In their rush to increase their wealth, they become immeasurably poorer as they squander what was truly wealth and replace it with a shallow poverty of betrayal.

Similarly, personal heritage or inheritance may also be squandered. If one is lucky enough to have been born into a distinguished family, then one has a responsibility to continue with its traditions and pass them on to the next generation. And yet, very often we hear stories in the media of those born into such positions who behave disgracefully, showing not only a disrespect, bordering on contempt, for others but an alarming lack of intelligence. In such a way, the thread of personal heritage may easily be broken, sometimes after many generations.

Heritage is itself wealth. Indeed, the value of precious works of all sorts, left to us by our ancestors, is incalculable. If we make the mistake of seeing such artifacts simply as objects to be bought, sold and generally prostituted in order to make money, then we fail to understand or appreciate this wealth. Instead, we shall plummet into an intellectual poverty, as has happened many times at a national level throughout the history of our world. This dichotomy between perceived wealth and actual poverty is an interesting one and, the more we develop our global culture of greed, the poorer we shall become in real terms.

Individuals face the same dilemma. If they perceive their heritage purely in material terms and devote their lives to maintaining this perceived wealth, then it is unlikely that they will find the time to understand that which would truly enrich their lives. The materially poor may, in some respects, have an advantage in this context as they have less, in a material sense, to protect and thus may more easily focus on other things. As with St Francis, they may discover the true wealth of the natural world around them. To develop the wealth that comes with knowledge. To develop moral and spiritual understanding and wealth. In so doing, they may create a heritage for their own descendants that will be worth more than any inherited fortune.

Of Poverty and Wealth

4. Character

It may seem odd to discuss poverty and wealth in terms of character but, in fact, it is very relevant to the individual. We used to use the term 'a man of good character' to refer to someone who we considered trustworthy and morally sound. This remains very relevant, although sometimes it seems that such individuals are hard to find, especially in the realms of commerce and politics. Nevertheless, a character may be imbued with wealth or poverty depending upon the trajectory of life followed by the individual. Those who remain mean of spirit, who harbour jealousies or who are manipulative and inherently dishonest will impoverish their own character, sometimes to the point of moral and intellectual destitution. Those, on the other hand, who remain open of heart, compassionate and who strive to understand, will enrich their character and become wealthy of spirit. Furthermore, such wealth may be systematically accrued as we walk the path of life, learning and observing as we go. Such a wealth will be further enhanced, the more we share it with others. Indeed, this might represent a better use of the term 'commonwealth' as we share our benevolent thoughts, ideas and knowledge of this world with others, particularly the younger generation. Those who strive to do this may certainly be considered wealthy of character and this wealth will remain unaffected by their material wellbeing, their position within society and other such factors which people often associate with wealth.

Indeed, the materially poor may themselves be rich in character if they learn, understand and share their understanding, without expectation of reward or acknowledgement, with those around them. It may be posited that we have a duty to do this within our short tenure of life on Earth. Such an assertion may seem out of place in a materialistic world where individuals are taught, from primary school onwards, that the purpose of learning and acquiring knowledge is to 'get on in the world' and make money. Their every step is then steered towards this goal of making money. When choosing a profession for themselves, the primary consideration for most will be how much money they might earn from developing a particular expertise or acquiring particular qualifications. Actually, the promotion of this attitude is ultimately not in the best interests of civilisation as it will result in the wrong people moving into areas which, in fact, require a completely different set of skills and attitudes. We see this, for example, in the health care profession where many are now becoming pharmacists and doctors purely because it is a profitable pursuit. Similarly, people enter politics for the same reason, ensuring a glut of the very worst personalities guiding the affairs of nations. These are good examples of individuals being poor in character and that poverty having a negative affect upon society in general.

The other side of this particular coin of course is when individuals are inspired to follow a particular profession because they believe passionately in their calling. This results in individuals who naturally share their expertise and good character, whether they be doctors, nurses, teachers, priests, scientists or artists. When individuals are inspired in this way, they bring joy to others through their conviction, attention and wealth of character. Doctors who are thus imbued bring a peace and healing to their patients way beyond that which medicine alone could provide. Similarly, in other professions, those who are wealthy in character go beyond the mundane to make our world a better and more interesting place. The great artists, such as Beethoven, touch the hearts of generation after generation with their particular inspiration.

Nations may also develop an identifiable character which serves to differentiate them from other nations. This national character may also be wealthy or poor. Such degrees of wealth or poverty have little to do with a nations material wealth or political power, but are more to do with attitude. Currently, some of the most powerful and materially rich nations are actually quite poor with regard to their national character, producing masses of individuals who are readily identified and tainted by this character. Sometimes, such a national character is distinct, such as the all prevailing Nazis in Germany during the 1930s. Sometimes the national character is less distinct, at least at first glance, such as with modern day America, but is nonetheless well established beneath the surface. Of course, in each case, there are personal exceptions to the national rule. National characters have an affect upon civilisation overall. The overtly materialistic character of super-capitalist America has, for example, spread across the world and undoubtedly changed global society. Whether that particular character is wealthy or poor, the author will leave the reader to consider for themselves.

But characters can change, if there is a will to do so. The leopard may yet change his spots, with a little inspiration and determination. Change should of course be directed towards creating a wealth of character, by increasing our understanding and sharing that understanding with others. Change in the opposite direction will only result in a diseased character on its road toward poverty. This is true at both a personal, organisational and national level.

Of Poverty and Wealth

5. National Situations

We often think of nations in terms of their wealth. How often we hear phrases such as 'One of the richest countries in the world' and politicians like to speak of Gross National Product and other such phrases, all of which are to do with material wealth.

Of course, a country needs to be solvent and able to finance its various public services. This comes from taxation. But so much of this financial resource is wasted on obscenely high salaries and related benefits and expenses for politicians, that only a certain proportion is actually expended upon services and care for society. It is ironic that even those countries described as the richest in the world often have a huge national debt which, clearly, will never be settled. So how can they be described as rich? It is all a matter of political chicanery and corruption wherein vast amounts of money change hands, seemingly in no relation to the welfare of the country. Britain is an example of a country with a huge national debt, with fundamental services such as health care, education and transportation breaking down and yet, it gives away billions of pounds each year in foreign aid. How can this be? Why is this money not being spent on essential services at home? At the same time, the British government, against the wishes of its own citizens, insists on maintaining an 'open door' immigration policy, inviting tens of millions of people onto a small island which clearly cannot support such numbers. The result is chaos, with the breakdown of essential services, sky high prices and significant inflation, panic building programmes and more. And yet, political propaganda insists that Britain has a thriving economy.

One particularly dishonest and unfair deception made by the combination of the British banking world and the British Government, is the pretence that there has been no inflation over the past decade. This deception enables banks to pay virtually zero interest on savings while still maintaining high charges for their services. This has been one of the biggest confidence tricks in history and the targets have been ordinary, decent citizens.

The British situation has been mentioned as an example, but one could make similar observations about many countries. The concept of wealth seems to be focused entirely on material and monetary concerns, with the whole distorted and manipulated by politics. Describing a country as 'wealthy' or 'rich' has come to be fairly meaningless, even in financial terms. At least for some countries. Others really are wealthy although, often, that wealth resides in the hands of a minority.

In any event, when we speak of national wealth, we are obsessed by money and material wellbeing. To such an extent, that we have convinced ourselves that every economy must grow every year. If, for some good reason it doesn't grow in one particular year, we consider this an abject failure. At every budget period we expect that the economy should grow financially. Any passing five year old could no doubt point out the absurdity in expecting constant growth and, particularly, of striving to achieve constant growth at the expense of every other consideration. And yet, all capitalist countries, which constitutes most of the countries in the world, regardless of how they describe themselves, have this expectation of constant material growth. We have fallen into the trap of believing that constant material and financial growth represents stability. In fact, it probably represents the exact opposite as, in the pretence that surrounds assertions of growth, all manner of distortions, deceptions and outright lies enter into the associated politics. The Great Deception, as the author likes to refer to it, cannot persist forever. At some point, cracks will appear in economies based upon such deceptions and, eventually, they will crash. We have already seen this happen with some cities and, the situation with countries is no different.

When economies crash, it opens the door for potential dictators or outside influence to move in and seize control. This, in turn, can lead to conflict and wars, as we have seen before. And yet, we never seem to learn the lessons of history. But countries are governed by their particular political system and it is politics that weave a web of deception and often lead their countries down paths which, perhaps, citizens would not have chosen for themselves. All of this is largely because we think of national wealth in terms of monetary and material worth. This is necessary to some degree as we must sustain civilisation, making use of the technologies of the day, as has been the practice for generations. However, once we understand the level of funding necessary to do this, there is no need to push further. The problem is, for many countries in the 21st century, is that they don't know when to stop. The universal culture of greed creates a hunger for material wealth that is never satisfied and can never be satisfied. Consequently, while becoming more wealthy in material terms, they become poorer in cultural terms.

Culture is the other criterion by which we might measure national wealth. It is a factor developed over many, many generations, each one adding a new thread to the tapestry that represents national culture. If it is revered, nurtured and celebrated, it will develop its own incalculable value, rendering its nationals wealthy in a way that material wealth alone could never achieve. It may consist of the country's heritage in terms of its achievements, its contributions to science, its artistic artifacts and its architectural monuments. But these things are simply a reflection of the true culture which is imbued in the hearts and souls of the country's people. And this culture is developed from the moment human beings stepped onto the particular piece of land involved, until the present day. In some countries, this human culture has swung back and forth as different races have populated the country, by peaceful means or otherwise. Nevertheless, each incumbent regime will have added a little to the overall culture, weaving its own thread within the broader tapestry.

However, at any point in history the accrued culture may be effectively destroyed if there is no political will to maintain it. In some cases, not only is there no will to maintain it, but it is actively destroyed. Statues, priceless works of art, books, religious icons and architecture have all been lost to posterity by wilful destruction. Furthermore, the effects of warfare have so often taken their toll upon our cultural heritage and, consequently, culture itself.

Just as monetary and material wealth may be squandered, cultural wealth may also be squandered. Often this happens in direct proportion to the incessant drive for material wealth. They are two sides of an equation that, ultimately, must balance. Citizens of a particular country may choose to appreciate its wealth in either cultural or material terms. Those who are absorbed by the desire for material worth may suppose that their wealth might buy them an experience of culture, perhaps by frequenting the performing arts. But that will result in only a superficial understanding. To really absorb and appreciate culture, one must take the time and trouble to study and understand it.

The national situation is complex and constantly shifting in its detail. However, if wealth is not understood and supported in a cultural sense, then no amount of material wealth can compensate. Some countries have diluted their own culture, usually by selfish political actions, to a point of no return. They may then never be a wealthy country, no matter how much they pretend otherwise.

Of Poverty and Wealth

6. Industry

The very word 'industry' implies wealth in the minds of many. It will elicit mental pictures of large, prosperous manufacturing plants, the provision of fuel and energy, transportation and other such obvious things. In some respects, this is an apt association as a nation's wealth is often linked with its home industries, just as an individual's wealth may be linked with industry. In our modern world we align industry with commercial enterprise, within our broader culture of greed. We do not, for a moment, consider that industry may be directed in other, altogether more meaningful, directions.

The Industrial Revolution was truly a revolution, not only in technology but in attitude. The focus was squarely on using technology to promote commerce and make money. Furthermore, humans were subservient to the technologies being developed. For example, in textiles, there were some wonderful and ingenious ideas developed in order to facilitate mass production within mills. And yet, the complex machines still required human beings to operate them. At the time, such developments were welcomed as they provided employment for the swelling population. The railways were a big step forwards and similarly provided employment for a great many people. Steel, ship-building, mining technology and, later, the production of motor cars, all boosted industry and many fortunes were made accordingly.

The Industrial Revolution has never really stopped. It has shifted around the globe and moved into areas of technology which would not have been anticipated in the age of steam, but the concept is alive and well. The use of technology to produce products upon a grand scale and market these products across the world is stronger than ever today.

What has changed is the relationship between technology and working individuals. In particular,

Industry

the ratio of jobs provided to material output. With automation, we produce more and more with less and less human input. This ensures that large corporations can make even more money with less commitment to providing employment. In addition, we live in a world of service industries, which are not really industries at all, but which provide the potential for vast profits with little investment, as they have no real stock in trade. Then there are industries like the IT industry that have thrived upon dishonesty and restrictive practices, charging exorbitant prices for what is really nothing at all in terms of product. In recent years it has become commonplace to target the 'hobby' market, whether it be fishing, cycling, photography or similar, and inflate prices by orders of magnitude, usually based upon false technology premises. In many of these areas, there is an additional niche market for the super-rich, where prices bear no resemblance at all to costs or even utilised technology, with products simply made to look special in one area or another.

All of these are examples where industry has become synonymous with making often obscene profits from consumers in one way or another. Sometimes these consumers are governments or large corporations, sometimes they are individuals. It matters not to the provider, as long as they can cheat by charging much more than their service or product is actually worth. This is one thing when the product is a luxury item that is not essential, thereby allowing the consumer to choose to by it or not. However, when the same dishonest practice is applied to essential services such as power, water, basic foodstuffs and clothing, then this is another matter altogether, with industry acting like a predator upon ordinary, decent people.

This type of industry, the only one that big business and politics understands, creates material wealth for those providing it. It also creates jobs for many people, some of whom also become very wealthy in a material sense. Directors of these large supply organisations often become obscenely wealthy, with fortunes so large that they become meaningless. Still they continue to pay themselves ever larger salaries, even though they can never spend the resulting fortunes. These are the super-rich who buy meaningless, super expensive toys in order to make statements about their wealth. They believe that they are special because, mostly by dishonest practices, they have made a great deal of money.

Industry

Politicians often follow a similar ethic, charging enormous fees for public speaking engagements or for promoting organisations in a practice that is laughingly described as 'lobbying'. Similarly, some of the shallow 'celebrities' artificially created for the entertainment industry make considerable fortunes for doing essentially nothing.

This is not to say that we do not need industry. We do need industry and that industry needs to be profitable in order to reinvest and improve its output, whether that be tangible product or a service. However that, with perhaps a very few exceptions, is not what is happening. Products are becoming worse in real terms as the focus is entirely on bringing down costs and manufacturing more for less. In service industries, there is little or no investment in training with a glut of unskilled individuals providing poor service to consumers. The focus is entirely on lowering costs and maximising profits. Profits which are then paid in bonuses and huge salaries to a small number of individuals at the top.

All of this and more comes under the umbrella of industry. The term has come to mean the creation of material wealth, by hook or by crook, but mostly by crook. Those who become wealthy by such means are only wealthy in a material sense. In other respects they are usually rather poor. Poor in their understanding of humanity, poor in their acquired knowledge of the world, poor in their compassion, poor in their relationship with animals, poor in their appreciation of nature, poor in their understanding of civilisation and the nobler creations of mankind. To be materially rich, but shallow in understanding, compassion and intellect is, on balance, to be poor.

There is another kind of industry. The industry in which gentlemen and gentlewomen may express a passion for creating something special. This may be an outstanding work of art such as a painting, a sculpture or perhaps the composition of music or the written word. If this passion is pursued with no expectation of reward, other than the joy of creation, then the industry expended in following it is a noble industry which enriches the soul. If however, it is pursued with the sole aim of attracting wealth and celebrity, then it is worthless.

The artifacts which we like to admire in celebration of our historic heritage are often the work of

Industry

industrious individuals who simply wanted to create something beautiful or otherwise special. Their industry has enriched our world in a manner in which the vulgar, profit chasing industry of today never will. Sadly, their time has passed and there will never be another Beethoven, Mozart, Van Gogh, Rembrandt, Bernini, Michelangelo or Botticelli. Nevertheless, there remains scope for the passionate to create beautiful objects, works of art or specialist items such as musical instruments, clocks and so on.

This, almost underground industry of passion creates wealth of another kind. Firstly, it enriches the creator with the experience of creating something beautiful. It must always be beautiful, whether it be a painting or a work of mechanical engineering. Secondly, it enriches every person who subsequently owns the artifact in question, providing of course, that they appreciate it in the proper sense. Consequently, the industry expended in creation is repaid many times over in appreciation of the work. Consider the magnificent and beautiful work of Beethoven. It enriched the composer immeasurably as it served to create the life and soul of Beethoven the man. But think of the countless millions of others whose lives have been enriched by the beauty of Beethoven's work. In this sense, the industry of one man has created incalculable wealth of the best possible kind, in that it has enriched the souls of millions of human beings, no doubt inspiring many of them to better things. Perhaps the reader might think of others who have enriched their own lives through industry of a similar nature.

But the best industry of all, is industry in the sincere service of others. Those who devote their time to helping the sick or comforting the lonely are industrious in the best possible sense because their industry is providing an immediate benefit to someone in need. The same is true of those who help animals or protect our wild places and natural environments. Kindness is the most effective tool used in any industry. Its profits are legendary and multiply many times, enriching many in the process. And yet it costs nothing. There are no 'capital costs' and the business of humanity may be practised by anyone. It is a business which, if encouraged and nurtured, would make our world a much better place. It would enrich everybody, both suppliers and consumers, in ways in which our

Industry

shallow industries of profit seeking greed and pretence never could.

Perhaps then, it is time for us to consider industry in a different light. To differentiate between essential industries that maintain practical civilisation and other industries which supply, in our 21st century, a much needed sustenance to the soul. There is little point in creating material wealth in extremis for groups and individuals who are morally destitute. There are better industries to pursue and cultivate, with the possibility of creating untold wealth, in the hearts and souls of millions.

Of Poverty and Wealth

7. Accumulation

In life, we tend to accumulate things. All manner of things, from unwanted gifts, objects which are of little practical use and other paraphernalia, to ideas and attitudes. Whether what we accumulate makes us wealthy will no doubt depend upon what exactly we do accumulate. The accumulation of expensive possessions which, are themselves of little intrinsic value, except as indications of financial wellbeing, will not make us wealthy. Even the accumulation of beautiful objects which are valuable, will not make us wealthy as we shall simply be acting as custodians of them until they are inherited by a future generation. However, the appreciation of beautiful works of art, when we know their history, will certainly enrich our understanding. Such an appreciation may be cultivated whether or not we own the objects in question. For example, we may view beautiful paintings in an art gallery and appreciate their cultural worth, without having to own them ourselves. Similarly with architecture and objects of art and, of course, we may appreciate great works via the performing arts, such as ballet, opera and music.

From a material perspective then, it is not necessary to own beautiful things in order to appreciate them, although this does not stop us from appreciating the things that we do own. However, accumulating more and more, in a material sense, will not necessarily make us increasingly wealthy. But the accumulation of knowledge, understanding and compassion will undoubtedly enrich our lives. In this world in which we live, we have a wonderful legacy of civilisation, of which we may absorb only a certain amount within the time allocated to us. We may therefore choose to be selective with respect to what we focus upon and the intensity of that focus. For example, professional classical musicians must necessarily spend a great deal of time learning and practising their craft, in order to attain a certain level of skill. This means that they will have less time to follow other interests. However, the joy that their skills brings to both themselves and those for

Accumulation

whom they perform, will enrich their lives enormously. One might say the same for others who are passionate about their chosen endeavour, providing it is followed for the right reasons and not just as a means of making money. The accumulation of money allows us to accumulate material possessions, but these alone will not make us wealthy. Indeed, the opposite may well prove to be the case for many individuals.

The most valuable thing that we might accumulate throughout life is a store of human kindness. And this is a miraculous store for, the more we expend it in the service of others, the more exists in the store. Compassion for those in need, whether humans or animals is a wealth that never runs out and is never lost. It is, therefore, surely worthy of our cultivation.

The accumulation of friends and acquaintances may or may not enrich our lives depending upon how and why we accumulated them. Those who cultivate acquaintance purely in the expectation of some personal benefit to the liaison, will find no enrichment in the association. Those who acquire friends as a result of their kindness and good deeds will find that each such friendship brings contentment and enrichment to their own lives. The old saying 'a friend in need is a friend indeed' rings true in many a case, providing that the hand of friendship is extended without expectation of any acknowledgement or reward.

We might, if we are unfortunate or careless, also accumulate bad habits that will impoverish our souls and, therefore, our life on Earth. This may especially be the case if we seek to emulate others for the wrong reasons. Many youngsters are effectively brainwashed by the razzle-dazzle of the material world, believing that it is their task in life to perpetuate the shallowness of the all pervading culture of greed which exists in the 21st century. They are taught, from an early age, the skills that will best enable them to do this and, unless they are particularly robust in character, there will be a tendency to blindly follow the herd in matters of taste, appreciation and behaviour. This is unfortunate as we are effectively bleaching out the ability to reason, and for individuals to think for themselves. Those who go with the flow will, by the time they are adults, have accumulated a glut of views and beliefs which are imprinted upon them from external sources, including the media and, of

Accumulation

course, peer pressure. For some, they realise this in good time and manage to unpick a lot of the views and assumptions imposed by their upbringing. Others may never do so and will continue to accumulate distorted perspectives, particularly in areas such as politics, religion and the all pervading culture of greed. A few may become confused and resort to substance abuse and anti-social behaviour in reaction to something which, deep down, they feel to be wrong, and yet do not quite understand.

Accumulation also affects nations of course, both in a material and cultural sense. From a material perspective, most nations strive to develop material wealth via industry and trade. Governments produce all manner of complicated reports to give the impression that the economy of the country in question is sound, whether it is or not. In any event, they simply raise taxes every year to generate more funds which they then squander on pointless initiatives, inflated salaries and, in some cases, foreign aid, for all the wrong reasons. Logically, there is no reason for a continual increase in taxes, but governments have got away with creating the expectation that they will rise, in real terms, every year and no one seems to question this now. Taxes may take many forms from direct taxation to taxation on goods, or simply the removal or downgrading of public services. The net effect is to provide more funding for politicians to abuse and abuse it they will, with unbridled vigour. An excess of material wealth is not good at the national level, just as it is not good at a personal level. In each case, the focus on material wealth bringing poverty in other areas.

At a national level, real wealth is contained in culture and the abilities of the population to both understand and create that which feeds into this culture. In order for that to happen, there must be a healthy degree of national pride among the population. A cosmopolitan, mixed race mishmash, thrown together simply to create material wealth will dilute the host culture to a degree which negates national pride and consequently erodes culture. We can see this happening in various countries where the population are brainwashed into not taking pride in their country or its past and are, instead, actively encouraged to denounce any form of what is described as nationalism, as if it were a crime. This has happened in Britain and the country is undoubtedly the poorer for it. Another

Accumulation

example of accumulating bad habits and character traits at a national level where, in fact, we should be striving for precisely the opposite effect. There are many other negative traits that a country may accumulate, one of the worst being corruption. This has spread like a disease throughout the world as both governments and large corporations have become increasingly corrupt. Often, the two work in harness in order to perpetrate crimes against humanity which, just a few decades ago, would have been considered intolerable. Acceptance of corruption is corruption itself, as it consolidates and validates the platform from which further corruption may be launched.

Our grandfathers and great grandfathers would be horrified to witness the practices which have become acceptable today in both commerce and politics. We have accumulated one layer of dishonesty after another in our facilitation of the culture of greed which seems to have the whole world within its dreadful grip.

Its time then, that we started to accumulate some more desirable traits including a higher level of education for the majority, the care of our natural world, a more caring attitude in society and the encouragement of real values and skills. All of these things may be systematically enhanced, layer by layer, generation by generation, developing a better world for future generations. However, we must have a plan to work to. A template for a better society, worked on and burnished by our best minds and implemented by far sighted government.

In such a manner, we may rid ourselves of negative accumulations and set our course for the accumulation of real wealth at both the individual and national level, banishing the cultural poverty that currently exists in so many of the worlds wealthiest countries. But only if we have the will to do so.

8. Education

Education is so important, a fact realised by ancient civilisations thousands of years ago. They realised that by providing education they provided understanding and, where appropriate specific skills, both of which enriched the life of the individual. Consequently, individuals performed their tasks or trade with pride and took satisfaction in doing so, not necessarily for material gain, but for the pride in a job well done. When we marvel at the remarkable achievements of, for example, the ancient Egyptians, we can appreciate the part that proper education and training played in those achievements.

In modern times, we associate education primarily with the means to make money. Individuals often pursue a particular academic thread purely on the basis of how much money they can make when properly qualified as a lawyer, doctor, accountant or some other profession. Even worse, the attainment of the relevant qualifications has become more important than a deep understanding of the subject at hand. This is now reflected in our secondary schools where emphasis is placed purely on passing exams, not on acquiring understanding or knowledge. Private, fee paying schools, are quite blatant in their advertising as being able to steer students through to passing exams. Even universities are seeming to dumb down the requirements for degrees and post graduate study. Often, students hardly attend the lectures and focus upon just writing up a thesis for their degree, much information for which they can glean from the Internet with very little study on their own part. The proof of the assertion made above may be found in the poor calibre of so called 'qualified' individuals coming out into industry.

To view education purely as a means to an end in financial terms is not only to miss the point from an individual perspective, but to betray the continuity of knowledge that has been built up during the course of civilisation itself. How can we add to this knowledge if we distort the very reason for its existence? Certainly we devise new abilities in areas such as software development, but much of this is to do with peripheral activities such as computer games or unneeded functionality and focused squarely on making money. This is not knowledge in the pure sense, but artfulness for inherently dishonest purposes, as so ably demonstrated by the leading IT organisations. Similarly with the design of goods and materials for the hobbyist markets where a constant churn of relatively useless gadgets are marketed at absurd prices in order for the supplying companies to grow as rich as possible as fast as possible.

One could provide a thousand more such examples. However 'education' designed to further such activities may support the generation of material wealth but does not add to the commonwealth of human knowledge and understanding. This is precisely why we live in a world governed by greed and deception. And just look at the mess it is in. Constant quarrelling and wars for no good purpose while we destroy our natural habitats hand over fist and betray our own history. The trajectory that this has brought us to is, ultimately unsustainable. We know this, and yet still we forge ahead with our unintelligent, contrived policies in support of nothing worthwhile. If our purpose on Earth is as caretakers for future generations, then we have failed miserably. The reasons for our failure are to be found in our incessant greed and the intolerance of anything that does not support The Great Deception. We have even allowed this deplorable attitude to taint education and align it simply with the acquisition of material wealth. This is perhaps the ultimate poverty as it robs people of the legacy of humanity. In this respect, many of our Neolithic ancestors were far wealthier than we are.

We could change this and turn things around by focusing upon true education whereby we teach people to understand. Not just the sciences and humanities as we perceive them today, but a much deeper understanding of life on Earth. More to the point perhaps, an understanding of how we might sustain life on Earth. In order to achieve this, we must cultivate a completely different level of intelligence, based upon reason. We must grapple with difficult concepts such as the explosion of human population and the need to introduce some form of intelligent control over this before the problem overwhelms us. We must understand that the consumption of natural resources must be aligned with their potential for replenishment. We must learn to cast aside the archaic concepts which have served to divide mankind for no good reason. We must learn to appreciate and preserve all life on Earth and understand that other animals are simply our brothers and sisters within the broader kingdom of life, and are thus entitled to the same consideration..

The acquisition of this knowledge would imbue us with a wealth far in excess of all the money and possessions in the material world, even were they multiplied a million times over. However, in order to bring this about, we must change the way we think about education. We must dispel this ludicrous concept that the purpose of education is to create wealth or to maintain a two tier society and replace it with an understanding that it is education alone that may enable the survival of the human species.

The education that we should be striving to provide would, of course, incorporate all that we have learned which is good and positive. The sciences in particular must receive a special focus. But we should also focus upon history and be able to learn from past mistakes, viewing them as stepping stones towards a greater intelligence. The Earth sciences should also be stressed in order to instil an understanding of the fabric of our world and the many natural mechanisms which maintain its special distinction within our galaxy. By bringing these strands together we may create a new science. The science of sustaining life on Earth in all its wonderful variation.

If we were to transform education in this way, with the focus shifted from greed to humanity and care of our beautiful planet, then we would have a blueprint for action. A blueprint of responsibility which would be imprinted upon young minds, enabling them to pursue meaningful careers which, in turn, will imbue them with real wealth. The wealth of understanding, knowledge and a life spent practising responsibility and compassion. Imagine the positive effect that a group of such individuals might bring to bear. Imagine the effect that a thousand such individuals might have. Imagine the effect that an entire generation of individuals educated in this manner might have upon our world.

Education

Some might view such a suggestion as an impossible dream. Many would scoff and say that this is far removed from reality and that the shallow greed culture that we currently embrace is simply human nature. But it is not human nature and the dream is not an impossible one. Indeed, if one has the foresight and integrity to look ahead objectively and extrapolate our current position along the trajectory being followed, it will quickly become apparent that this position is not sustainable. Consequently, the 'impossible dream' becomes an absolute requirement if human civilisation is to continue.

The current global culture of greed and deception is a culture of poverty. Poverty of understanding, poverty of appreciation and poverty of compassion. If we are to throw off the shackles of this poverty we need to start with education. Not as it is currently expressed, but with a renewed purpose, such as is suggested within these pages. A new movement. A new deal for humanity. Who will have the courage to make a start?

Of Poverty and Wealth

9. Appreciation

For many, if not the majority in this world, appreciation has been distorted into a vulgar appreciation of material wealth. A shallow appreciation of all that glitters artificially and of equally shallow celebrity. This is ironic given the wonderful legacy of art, science and literature that civilisation has left us. If we had ten lifetimes we could never explore it all and yet, so often, one comes across adults who have never read a serious book, claim that they hate classical music and understand nothing about history, geography and humanity, let alone the sciences. Such individuals often have highly paid jobs and are convinced that they must therefore be very special, so why bother with all that heritage rubbish. Of course, they do not realise how fragile their position really is until, one day, it comes to an abrupt end, and then they are lost because they do not have the grounding that a broader education and appreciation provides. Those that appreciate nothing but money and material wealth are indeed living in poverty. And poverty of appreciation is indeed a dreadful thing as it robs the soul of so much.

Those who cultivate a gentle appreciation of all things, past and present, develop a wealth of mind that cannot be destroyed by unexpected events. The more they appreciate about life and humanity, the stronger their inner constitution becomes. And it is not just about our remarkable legacy of knowledge, but the appreciation of the moment. The natural world in all its wonder and our relationships with both our fellow humans and other forms of life. There is so much that is wonderful and beautiful in our world. It is almost a sin not to absorb and appreciate as much of it as possible during our brief time on Earth.

One of the issues with contemporary life is the erosion of standards and the subsequently distorted values which affect the lives of so many across the world. We are reminded constantly that we live in

Appreciation

the age of technology and therefore have to consume as much of it as possible, whether or not it is actually of any particular value. An example of this is the curious way in which mobile phones and tablet computers have been so strongly marketed that almost everyone, even in so called third world countries, uses them. But for what? Playing with these devices absorbs so much time that those who become addicted to them have little spare time for anything else. The manner in which people seem glued to their mobile phones, even when walking down the street or travelling on a bus or train, ensures that they cannot appreciate anything else which is occurring around them. They miss everything, from the beauty of the day and whatever glimpse of nature they might see, to the pleasure of interacting with others around them. Indeed, as many others have commented, these technologies are anti-social in that they erode the natural tendency for people to speak with each other. Indeed, that social dialogue, even at the mundane chit-chat level, is actually very important as it serves to weld people together into a community. Some might argue, with some justification, that we are creating on-line communities via social networking web sites, but it is hardly the same thing. Interaction via social networking sites is both passive and, if the user wishes, anonymous. There is no direct interaction and one cannot read and respond to the emotions of a human being when you cannot see them. Neither can you appreciate the subtle nuances which make live, physical interaction so interesting. In fact, what we are creating with social networking web sites is not communities, but simply collections of files which are posted on a web server somewhere, by individuals who may or may not be who they claim to be.

To rely solely upon electronic communication is to impoverish the art of human interaction. An art which, until recently, had flourished for thousands of years. Technology, in the form of computer games has a similarly anti-social effect as it absorbs significant amounts of time which might otherwise be spent liaising and interacting with other individuals. This is particularly tragic when it occurs within the family causing family members to be effectively estranged from one another.

In the so called 'age of technology' we may be

Appreciation

enriched by certain technologies if they support health care, or otherwise serve to enhance the quality of life for the majority. However it does not necessarily follow that technology is always a good thing. Technology can also serve to impoverish us, as in the illustrations provided herein.

Appreciating this distinction is important. On one hand technology may be synonymous with wealth, on the other hand it may reflect poverty. This is especially the case when it impacts upon human relationships. It is a poor man who does not appreciate the value of human interaction. The joy of conversation, compassion shown in everyday situations and the complex relationships between individuals. These are all things to be savoured.

It is also a poor man who does not appreciate nature. The wonder of evolution and the beauty to be found in the natural world, enrich the soul with an understanding of life that cannot be found in the material world alone, and certainly not on a mobile phone. Walking on a wind-swept moor, climbing on the fells, drinking from a mountain stream, and interacting with animals in the wild represent a wealth of experience that cannot be diminished or lost. But in destroying natural habitats for purposes of commercial gain, we at once squander this wealth and impoverish both ourselves and our descendants. And it is not just terrestrial landscapes which we are destroying, but the oceans as well, with our deep sea drilling, noise pollution and the dumping of waste, all of which is having a devastating effect upon marine life. Add to this the problem of over fishing which exists, more or less all over the world, and the survival of our oceans and the life they support also come into question. The same is happening on land and, of course, in the atmosphere, all of which are inter-connected within a very complex web of interactions and dependencies. By plundering these natural resources for commercial gain, we think we are creating wealth when, in fact, we are creating poverty. This lack of appreciation of the natural world may well prove to be disastrous for the human species.

It may be argued that, throughout history, we have appreciated the natural world in our art, both in paintings, architecture, literature and music. There may be truth in such an argument, but how may we appreciate it in the future if it is irrevocably

Appreciation

damaged? If we destroy our natural landscapes, we shall not be able to reflect them in art. We are already losing species at an unprecedented rate through what might prove to be a mass extinction. We are no longer able to appreciate those species which have already disappeared, except via historic imagery. Is that to be the fate of the natural world? And how might that enrich us? It will not. In fact, it might destroy us, as we are an integral part of nature and depend upon it, including its various complex interactions and dependencies absolutely. Consequently, appreciating this fact may be pertinent to our own survival.

An appreciation of the natural world and evolution is essential if we are to manage our world. Indeed, to acquire such an appreciation is to acquire real wealth. Monetary wealth, in comparison, means nothing. Even as an individual we may acquire this natural wealth, by reading, observing and learning. And this wealth continues to grow as we get into the habit of learning and caring for our world.

Similarly, an appreciation of life itself and a compassion for all living things creates its own wealth within our hearts. A wealth that can never be diminished no matter how hard our experience of life might be. We would do well to express this appreciation, to all those around us, and especially those who, themselves, share their own kindness and compassion. The old adage that there is good in everyone is mostly true. The most odious rogues often turn out to have a soft spot that causes them to do good in one area or another.

And so, appreciation is another area where we might become wealthy or poverty stricken, depending upon our focus and the time we are prepared to invest in appreciation of that which is truly valuable, as opposed to that which is frivolous and meaningless.

10. Creativity

Creativity is not limited to the human species but may be witnessed among many animals and, of course, nature itself in all its wondrous creations. We may think of it as creating something that was not there previously, either by alteration or by starting from scratch. From ancient times, the human species has been particularly creative as it has sought to bend nature to its own requirements.

Much of what has been created by humanity, particularly in the arts, has bestowed a particular kind of wealth. The great paintings, sculptures, music and literature have enriched the lives of us all throughout the ages. Our lives would certainly be poorer without Beethoven, Rembrandt, Dickens and the many others who have contributed to this quite wonderful commonwealth of intellectual creativity.

Similarly, in the sciences, we have created wondrous mechanisms and made countless discoveries which, together, have enriched our lives over the millennia, adding to our understanding of the world in which we live.

When creativity is exercised in a positive sense, such as described, then certainly it creates its own wealth and, mostly, this is a wealth that may be enjoyed by the majority. Unfortunately, creativity may also be used in a negative sense, to create weapons of mass destruction, to create policies that discriminate and persecute, to create predatory commercial and political models that exploit populations, to create propaganda that effectively dumbs down the majority and eliminates the ability to reason among the majority. When used in this manner, creativity can create intellectual, moral and sometimes physical poverty.

We may also exercise creativity in our relationships with others. By creating tolerance, compassion and understanding within ourselves, we may exercise kindness in our personal relationships which, in turn, will create its own form of wealth which may be enjoyed among all those with whom we come into contact. This sort of relational wealth is infectious and, once instigated, can spread positively among entire groups of individuals, enriching all of their lives accordingly. Imagine if everyone were to practice this positive relational creativity. The world would surely be a much happier and more benevolent place.

Just as relational creativity may be employed positively, it may also be practised negatively, bringing sadness and distress to many people. Those who bear false witness or go out of their way to persecute another spread a form of creative evil. This creative evil can also spread and come to affect a great many people, as we have seen throughout history, right from biblical times, where those with vested interests sought to persecute and divide to their own advantage, often under the cover of religion or politics. During the second world war, the Nazis were especially creative, not only in furthering the mechanisms of war and building their infrastructure, but in the persecution and elimination of those that they saw as their political and cultural enemies. Their creativity certainly changed the world and, had it not been for brave resistance of relatively few at the critical time, it may have changed it even more. Today, even in times of relative peace, the negative creativity of politicians is changing the world even more than the Nazis could have dreamed of, and the impact upon ordinary, decent people is just as dramatic, albeit in different ways.

In matters of education we have allowed our negative creativity to replace inspiration and real knowledge with computers and an emphasis on popular culture, even to the point of disallowing history and proven scientific concepts. This ensures that we breed generations with little respect for the past and with even less capacity for reason. This, in turn, perpetuates the negative creativity of the greed culture where nothing seems to matter except making money. Even in the sciences, we have allowed negative creativity to contribute to The Great Deception where opinions and propaganda have replaced true scientific thought. A good example of this is the industry that has been created around the notion of climate change, something which would be happening whether we were here or not as the Earth continues its exit from the last ice age. Meanwhile, true innovations in environmental thinking, such as Evolutionary Conservation, are studiously ignored even though they offer the opportunity for positive creativity in the way we might protect natural habitats and better manage our natural resources.

We are constantly brainwashed into believing that all this negative creativity is creating wealth when, actually, it is rendering us more poverty stricken than we have ever been in certain respects. As a result, we are engulfed in a poverty of understanding, a poverty of reason and a poverty of compassion such as the world has rarely known.

One might suppose that our creativity remains strong in the artistic sense, but does it? Just look at the rubbish which is passed off as art these days. Abstract creations which display no particular skill and absolutely no humanity. People often ask why there has never been another Beethoven or Mozart, or Rembrandt or Titian, or Dickens or Shakespeare. It is because of our poverty of creativity, brought about by a dumbing down of education, appreciation and a parallel surge in negative creativity overall. Meanwhile The Great Deception has convinced the masses that we live in the technological age and that, therefore, we have never had it so good. We boast about the high number of millionaires and billionaires that our societies have created. An artificial wealth based upon exploitation and propaganda. But where is the wealth of understanding, of compassion, of humanity? It exists among a dwindling population of those who have been strong enough to reason for themselves and resist the propaganda. You will not find them among the plethora of shallow celebrities or among politicians or captains of industry. This is ironic as it is they who hold the key to the salvation of humanity.

The objective of every thinking person therefore should be to engage in positive creativity in all that they do. In their relationships and in their life's work, whatever their calling might be. For it is in that positive creativity that they will find true wealth. A wealth that can never be found among the glittering material possessions of delusions of importance that accompany those who embrace negative creativity for purposes of their own.

11. Understanding

Those who devote their whole lives to the accumulation of material wealth will have no time or room in their thoughts for any deeper understanding. We hear so many times how those in positions of power state quite emphatically that there is nothing as important as making money. They consequently spend their lives pursuing this goal and, if asked about a deeper intellectual subject, perhaps in the arts or sciences, will have no opinion on the matter. They will have no opinion because they have no understanding, and they have no understanding because they have never given any time or thought to such matters. They are, in fact, intellectually poverty stricken, no matter how much wealth they surround themselves with. That is not to say that the materially wealthy cannot harbour intellectual gifts or appreciate deeper matters, but that the endless pursuit of material wealth above all else shuts out any deeper understanding of life. We see this also in those career politicians who become infatuated with what they believe is power, devoting their whole lives to manipulation and, where necessary, deception. They also have no time to cultivate a deeper understanding of life and are correspondingly poor as a result, no matter how much they reward themselves financially. There are some very good examples of this syndrome within our current generation.

The sort of understanding that generates true wealth needs to be cultivated and takes time. It is typically accumulated over a lifetime of dedication to the task, providing incremental benefits along the way. It starts with education, both at home and at school. Education is the key to the treasure chest of understanding that has been built up by our ancestors. Thousands of years of civilisation across multiple cultures have provided us with a cornucopia of heritage, including the wisdom that has accumulated throughout all of that time. A life spent without acknowledging and embracing that heritage is a life spent in error. Even one lifetime is hardly enough to absorb that font of knowledge and ideas, let alone accumulate one's own store of understanding.

Nevertheless, those that do make this effort will be enriched beyond measure. It will be their task to understand and to add a little to this understanding for future generations, thus creating a wealth of ideas and heritage that is in place for all those who can see it. And it is not just an understanding of past events and knowledge that is important, but to add to this an understanding of current global situations and to be able to place these within a proper context. The individual who has a good grasp of all these things will enjoy a wealth that cannot be lost or eroded by external influence or events, no matter how severe.

In addition, one must cultivate an understanding of, and empathy with, other people, regardless of their own background or culture. While it is true that those of a different culture will harbour different beliefs, ideas and, very often, moral codes, there nevertheless exists much which is common across all humanity. Being able to see and, when necessary, speak to these common facets of humanity is a skill well worth developing. Such a skill will enrich the understanding of the individual concerned while simultaneously reaching out to others and helping to spread this understanding further afield. One might think of this as both generating and distributing a wealth of the very best kind.

Those who sacrifice the acquisition of this understanding of humanity for the pursuance of material wealth engage in an enterprise in which they are undoubtedly the loser. One occasionally hears of materially rich individuals who, for one reason or another, lose their fortunes entirely, sometimes along with everything they have. Occasionally, these individuals suddenly realise the shallowness of material wealth and come to understand how much time they have wasted in its pursuit. They then often switch dramatically to the acquisition of an understanding of humanity, occasionally devoting the remainder of their lives to a good cause. While it is always comforting to see an individual come to such an understanding, it is a pity that they have to arrive at it in such a manner. How much easier it would be if they were taught such an understanding from childhood and were

Understanding

able to embrace it throughout their entire lives. It follows then that education systems should include an understanding of humanity within their various curricula, together with an understanding of the arts and sciences. If this were pursued with passion and inspiration, our youngsters would be leaving the education system with a ready store of a wealth of understanding, to which they could add in future years.

Imagine if this was already in place. What a difference it would make to our professionals and politicians. Those who become doctors and health care professionals would exercise a proper duty of care towards patients before worrying about their own salaries or terms and conditions. Those in industry might consider how their goods and services benefit the community rather than simply extorting as much money as possible from citizens. Politicians might, for once, start to consider the welfare and future of the countries they are presiding over. The reason none of these things happen today is partly due to our distorted values and the corruption that they induce within those involved. Corruption, left unchecked, goes further to create indifference and incompetence upon a wide scale as may be readily witnessed in countries such as Britain, a once proud and distinguished nation now reduced to a shambles infused by a huge swathe of asylum seekers and illegal immigrants who have no understanding of the country's history and achievements. This gross distortion has been inflicted upon the country by politicians who, now unable to balance the books because of the gigantic welfare induced debt, are now closing down hospitals, one after another, withdrawing funding from schools and local authorities and generally dumbing down everything. Simultaneously, they have increased foreign aid as part of the corrupt mechanism that ensures the material wealth of those involved. The irony is that our so called 'leaders of nations' spew out such a lot of nonsense about strong economies and wealth when, in reality, they impoverish the countries whose administration they are entrusted with. Britain is an excellent example of this, although other countries are similarly afflicted by the disease of corruption and incompetence. What sort of wealth is this creating? And for whom? No doubt there are small pockets of individuals, such as property developers, bankers, energy suppliers and others in Britain, who are making substantial fortunes at the expense of the wellbeing of the community. But this is material wealth borne of corruption and is consequently meaningless within the broader scheme of things. What good is this in the face of societal and cultural poverty? It could all so easily be different if we encouraged and nurtured a different sort of understanding, imbued at childhood and practised in life.

Even ancient civilisations had a better grasp of this than we do today. The ancient Egyptian mythology created a beautiful understanding among its children of justice and character. Their belief in training and education ensured that they were able to achieve remarkable feats, not just in monumental architecture, but in all practical fields of everyday life. Consequently, they managed to keep their society working for thousands of years, their understanding ensuring that things functioned according to plan and for the benefit of all. The modern world should have learned much from their example, instead, we often ridicule them as a stagnant civilisation. Actually, nothing could be further than the truth. Compare Pharaohs such as Senwosret 1st in the Middle Kingdom with our current leaders of nations. Well, there is no comparison. Senwosret lead from the front and worked hard throughout his life for the common good of Egypt and the welfare of the community. The same was true of Senwosret 2nd and Senwosret 3rd. Amenhotep 1st similarly worked hard for his country and brought many benefits to all Egyptians. These leaders understood both the past and the present in relation to their country. A country which they loved with all their hearts and strove to protect and improve. Can we say that of our own leaders? Certainly not in modern Europe.

This misunderstanding of what constitutes real wealth in the community has caused hugely significant and largely irreversible damage to countries who, in fact, had distinguished histories. None more so than Britain. Is this to be the way of the world? One can only hope not as, if this were so, it would mean that civilisation itself is receding at an alarming rate. That, in turn, would not bode well for the survival of humanity. Is it too late to turn things around? Maybe not, but there would have to be a revolution of thought in order for this to take place. Such a revolution might be painful and might even create conflict among nations. Such may be the price of advancement. One thing is certain and that is that the current wave of corruption, incompetence and indifference is not sustainable. It is already resulting in the breakdown of infrastructure and a notable worsening of important factors such as education and health care. Such a trajectory cannot be maintained indefinitely. A new understanding must be sought, developed and practised.

Our obsession with material wealth and the making of money has impoverished our society in real terms. How much longer must we tolerate such a distortion of values and understanding?

12. Morality

In our modern world, people scoff at the very mention of the word 'morality' as if were something to be avoided at all costs. So often, we hear politicians, businessmen, educators, broadcasters and others claim proudly that morality doesn't feature in anything that they do. They are afraid, even of the word. The same is true of many in the health care profession and in other pursuits that affect the lives of so many others. And yet, surely, morality should be the cornerstone upon which all our endeavours are founded. Without morality we are existing in a wilderness of seediness and corruption. Within such a wilderness, material wealth is in fact shallow and meaningless. It is imperative, if humanity is to survive, that we find a road out of this wilderness. Morality is the signpost that will set us upon the right path and lead us towards a righteous wealth that benefits the commonwealth of mankind.

However, words are just words. What we need is positive action. Action which ensures that morality is taught in schools, from primary schools, through secondary schools and on to higher education. It should be the backbone of all our universities, ensuring that all courses and paths of study are imbued with a moral context. Consequently, by the time an individual has progressed through the education system, he or she should have a firm moral basis, underpinning all of their thoughts and future activities.

In such a manner, this moral context would then find its way into industry, into the professions and even into government. Yes, imagine a government whose policies reflected a moral responsibility to society. How different such a government would be and how more efficient and meaningful would its administration become. With morality, we also encourage justice, as the two are inseparable. And justice is the keystone of any responsible

Morality

administration. Without justice, administrations falter and invite challenges, often with disastrous results as all history shows. A moral and just administration is the only form of government that can ever provide real wealth. Anything else is likely to reduce a nation to moral and intellectual poverty, as has been happening throughout Europe and the world in recent decades.

The same is true at an individual level. Those who base their lives upon morality, justice and therefore compassion, will generate their own wealth, irrespective of their position within society. Those who abandon such principles for the sake of making money or achieving status, will spend their lives in moral and spiritual poverty, often only realising the fact right at the last moment, when it is too late to change.

But, of course, it is individuals who make up governments and who run large corporations and these same individuals who bring their own lack of morality to bear upon their actions and intentions in office. This is precisely why such large corporations and governments are so hideously corrupted. They bask in their own shallow wealth and false celebrity, believing that they have made something of their lives. Their arrogance, knowing no bounds, leads them to believe that they are successful in life, by dint of their own intelligence, which they believe to be superior to that of those whom they so ruthlessly exploit. They believe that dishonesty is simply an acceptable way of conducting business in the 21st century. Politicians, guided by their corrupt and dishonest mentors, openly lie about everything, believing that this is now acceptable within the modern world. Those who are particularly devious believe that they are more intelligent than their slightly less devious fellows.

What a sad indictment of the human race. Have we really come so far, over thousands of years of civilisation, to such a sorry conclusion? A global society devoid of morals, with the administration of nations based upon treachery and open dishonesty. Large corporations who act immorally and dishonestly as though this were something to be proud of. And societies foolish enough to place those who are most successfully immoral and dishonest upon pedestals, creating shallow celebrities and rewarding them accordingly. Even the public honours systems in most countries have become so corrupted that the awarding of such honours has become almost something to be pitied, especially when politically motivated. Our sense of values has become so distorted that we are producing immoral and dishonest robots by the million and depositing them upon the world. Where will this lead us? We have already witnessed the wanton destruction of all that was noble and good. Concepts such as morality, nobility of spirit and dignity are openly ridiculed, by politicians, by the media and by so called celebrities. The power of the connected world amplifies the atrocity, for that is what it is, and betrays successive generations into believing that such attitudes are acceptable and, indeed, inseparable from success.

If we continue in this vein, we shall be destructing, piece by piece, all the advances of humanity accomplished throughout past millennia. We shall be disallowing all that was good, kind and necessary for human beings to live contented and meaningful lives. The tragedy, and it is a tragedy, is the speed with which this is happening. If we look back 60 or 70 years we witness communities who may not have had some of the technical conveniences of today, and yet who were obviously much happier. Societies where there was no need to have 'police states' governed by restrictive legislation and regulation. Where neighbours knew and supported each other within communities which were safe and where everyone found their particular place and were contented with it. These were societies where morals were still regarded as important. If we go back even further we find that, conflicts excepted, there were even stronger codes of decency and honour based upon moral underpinnings. Such times are often described as 'innocent'. If by 'innocent' we mean less corrupted and immoral, then so be it. In any event, we were much closer to the concept of humanity and what it means to be a human being.

The reader may readily appreciate the importance of morality when the case is so put. So why have we abandoned it so ruthlessly within our modern way of life? What has been our reward for such a drastic realignment of values? It seems that the only reward has been to make a minority of the population super rich, by allowing predatory and dishonest practices in both commerce and government. Given the shallowness of the wealth thus created, it hardly seems like a good bargain. But still we brainwash

Morality

our younger generations to believe that the only thing important in life is to make money. And to make money by whatever means are available, whether honest or not or whether moral or not. A society that ridicules morality is a poor society indeed. A society steeped in poverty of the worst kind. It is surely time for a change. A time to embrace morality and to restore spiritual wealth to our global community. Failure to do so will spell the end of civilisation as we have known it.

13. Generosity

The terms 'generosity' and 'wealth' do not always sit comfortably together, as material wealth is so often associated with meanness and artful corruption. Whereas the opposite is true of spiritual wealth, as this is readily shared with others through a generosity of spirit that would seem alien to the materially wealthy. Those who are generous, especially when they have little enough to give except their time and compassion, are truly wealthy as they receive back many times what they expend in human kindness. And this personal generosity is not only about giving, but about simply being there and understanding when those around you need your presence, for whatever reason. It follows then that the generous must also be perceptive. They must sense when and where their generous support is needed and respond accordingly. This may be relatively easy among family, work colleagues and those to whom you are close on a day to day basis, but the truly generous will extend this understanding and perception to total strangers, if they are in need. This is a natural form of generosity which we, and most of the animal kingdom, are born with and should thus be easily exercised.

Unfortunately, this form of natural generosity is often systematically bleached out of the individual by immersion in the material world. Those who are weak in spirit and personality are easily turned and corrupted by the universal culture of greed which teaches them to grab as much for themselves as quickly as possible, and to hang on to it at all costs. We regularly hear assertions such as "if you don't take it, no one is going to give it to you" and "it is your life, you must put yourself first and look after number one". That such statements are made, and often made, in all seriousness is a sad indictment of what humanity has become.

Living for others and sharing your life and whatever talents you might have freely with others reflects a generosity of spirit that will be repaid a thousand times over, creating a level of inner wealth

Generosity

that those who crave material wealth will never attain. They will instead spend their lives in poverty of the worst kind. Poverty of the soul.

Some of those who, by hook or by crook, have attained material wealth, will often attempt to assuage their conscience by giving a small amount to charity (and just as often boast about it). This is not generosity at all. It is simply self appeasement. In addition, it is a sad fact that many charities these days are not charities at all, but businesses, with large corporate structures of highly paid executives. Consequently, the majority of their funding goes to perpetuate this model. Indeed, heads of charities have become one of the most sought after positions for those who wish to make their material fortunes. It is a particular distortion of the greed culture in which we live.

The truly generous individual will give directly of his or her time and, perhaps, some material or practical aid, only where they can see that it is needed. They will generally do so incognito and would certainly never boast about it. Furthermore, for them, it will not be an isolated, one-off instance, but a matter of continual support for those around them who need, for whatever reason, and in whatever form, their kind assistance. And this assistance, while taking many forms, will rarely be in direct financial aid, as that, very often serves no purpose in itself. However, they may expend their own finances on behalf of those being helped.

And so, personal generosity is inseparable from the natural generosity of spirit that is embedded into our soul at birth. If we have allowed it to become distorted and withered by greed, envy and selfishness, then we must reverse this process and nurture it back to health, as we would do with a dying flower. When it is back in bloom, its beauty will shine and spread from within to all those with whom its bearer comes into contact.

Just as there is such a thing as personal generosity, there is also communal generosity and even generosity among the administration of nations, although the latter is rarely found these days. Communal generosity is very important and, just as with personal generosity, must come from the heart and must be freely shared without expectation of recognition or reward. It might be focused and embodied by an elected council, or by a looser gathering of individuals. In any event, it will be keen to ensure that there will be no unnecessary suffering within the community. This will include an awareness of the elderly who may not be able to fend for themselves, those afflicted by disease or disability and other such obvious causes. But it will also strive to provide a haven where anybody, for whatever reason, may gather, simply to be with other people and, perhaps to share either their talents or concerns.

Many communities have a Community Centre which, in essence, should be providing such services and many of them come close to doing so. Unfortunately, many of them are also organised along local government lines and are therefore more about supplying designated services than taking the time to listen and to understand. However, such official centres may be complemented by voluntary efforts, where the local authority allows, in order to enhance and broaden their scope. Sometimes, this can work quite well and, certainly, we should give every encouragement and support to such centres. This in no way limits our ability to create other services, and even public centres, where we perceive a need to do so. These might consist of a handful of volunteers coming together to provide transport for those needing to visit hospitals. Or perhaps a team who can come and help with house work when individuals become too frail to do so for themselves. Sometimes, it may be just coming and sitting with someone who has little or no day to day human contact and who craves companionship. There is so much that we can do within a defined community if we have a will to do so. And this should not be the preserve of the retired and elderly. Youngsters should also be encouraged to volunteer their time. Indeed, the reward in kind for youngsters may be that much greater as the experience may serve to change the course of their entire lives for the better. One may readily appreciate the power inherent in this type of generosity. It is so much more meaningful than simply 'giving to charity'.

National generosity is a much rarer thing and often, what poses as generosity, is not generosity at all, but a political mechanism whose aim is to extract some benefit from the target, usually natural resources, business interests or something similar. This is how foreign aid works. In every case, it has nothing to do with helping ordinary civilians within the target country, but is all about establishing business agreements, sometimes in setting up low cost manufacturing, sometimes in extracting minerals and natural resources, sometimes simply a matter of political manoeuvring. This has nothing to do with generosity as the giver is expecting a direct reward in return. This is precisely why the many billions of dollars poured into Africa over the years, for example, have had no obvious benefit for ordinary people. They have however made countless dictators super rich in the process. One could give many other such examples.

From a national perspective, one might well claim that generosity should start at home. If a given country is wealthy, then that wealth should be expended upon social services such as education and health care. It should be expended on creating a caring society of which the mother country may, with some justification, be proud. However, this rarely happens. More often, it is simply the politicians who become super rich, especially once they have reached ministerial, or premiership level. How sad that their corruption and ardent pursuit of material wealth impoverishes them so, in areas where it is really important. It need not be this way

Of Poverty and Wealth

of course. Even the Pharaohs in ancient Egypt, while enjoying the trappings of their Royal position, nevertheless took responsibility for the country and its people and strove to improve things for everyone. Was it not Amenhotep III who proclaimed upon taking office, two simple objectives; Firstly, that 'no man shall pull my bow' and secondly that, 'no one shall go hungry in my time'. He was right on both counts and, as a sign of grateful respect, when he died his bow was cut in two and laid beside him in his sarcophagus so that no man would ever pull his bow. But then he was a great leader. And his personal generosity of spirit enriched an entire nation.

In short, generosity creates wealth, among all those with which it is shared as well as the host. A lack of genuine generosity creates poverty. Not poverty of possession or of artificial importance, but real poverty. Poverty of the soul.

14. Meanness

There is perhaps nothing more damning or more destructive than meanness. It is at the root of the greed culture and everything within it, including false celebrity, corruption and that intolerable mixture of arrogance, ignorance and deception which seems to have engulfed so much of our modern world.

Meanness of spirit is therefore something to be avoided at all costs as it is an inhibitor of real wealth. There is a common misconception that meanness often comes from those who have had difficult backgrounds or who know what it is like to go without. But this is simply not the case. On the contrary, those from poorer backgrounds often develop compassion and generosity of spirit as they understand what is really important in life. No, meanness is more usually the product of greed. Greed and envy, as the mean covet the possessions or positions of others. In striving to emulate that which they envy, they become mean in spirit and in actuality as they try to manoeuvre themselves into a more desirable social position. Those who are self obsessed in this way will suffer from their own meanness much more than those to whom their meanness is directed.

We may witness meanness in all walks of life. From the purely social to the professional and, of course, in politics where it is rife. In every case it is a negative attribute which serves no one well. If a man is mean to his brother, what benefit does it bring to him? Perhaps some fleeting sense of material betterment, but at what cost? His reputation suffers irreparable damage that no amount of material wealth can compensate for. In addition the person to whom he shows his meanness is also hurt by the action. So no-one benefits and all are harmed. It is, in fact, a totally negative trait of character which we should strive to eliminate whenever we catch a glimpse of it.

Unfortunately, meanness is like an illness. It can be

contagious, especially among those who are easily influenced. If they witness what they see as material or social benefits in others which they attribute partly to their meanness, then they seem to readily accept the virus and behave likewise. But, like an illness, it harms the individual in question and often leaves a lasting mark on them.

Part of our education of children should focus upon the distinction between meanness and generosity and how the two attributes affect both the giver and receiver of both. It should be shown, by rational argument, that meanness has no part to play in a civilised and caring society and that the intelligent individual must studiously avoid it.

Many will of course scoff at any such suggestion and try to hold that meanness is simply human nature. Some sort of natural protection mechanism to ensure our survival. It is not. Neither is it among animals, many of whom demonstrate remarkable sensitivity and generosity towards their fellows, sometimes even across species. There is nothing natural about meanness. It is a negative side effect of a calculating mind. But such a mind is also capable of more positive attributes, such as kindness, compassion and generosity. So why not allow these positive attributes to prevail? it would so clearly be better for all concerned.

Another misconception is that it is necessary to be mean in order to become wealthy. In fact, the mean can never be wealthy, no matter how much they may possess. The distraction of constantly counting the cost of everything and the benefit of every situation to themselves, ensures that there is no room in their constitution for any other understanding. Consequently, they can never experience the wealth of true friendship, love, appreciation, knowledge or contentment. You would think that this should be obvious to every thinking individual, but clearly this is not the case. One only has to look at the global media, cinema and computer games to witness how obsessed we have become with meanness, violence and destruction. To the point that, astonishingly, we consider consideration of the same as entertainment. We have coined the term 'anti-hero' as an example to hold up to generations, as if to show that, somehow, meanness is a desirable way of life. And to prove the point, we award those who, through their meanness, have become 'successful' with every accolade that society permits. This is not the mark of intelligent civilisation. Furthermore, it is not a model that we should be recommending to younger generations. Those distorted and ugly media and entertainment channels could just as easily be portraying generous and noble deeds, and celebrating the kindness and compassion of humanity. Our civic reward systems could just as easily be rewarding the good and noble of spirit as the shallow celebrities with their equally shallow self obsession and meanness. And there are so many examples to be found of unselfish, generous spirits in society, if we really look for them. These should be the role models that we hold up for the young to emulate.

For those afflicted with the disease of meanness, one can only hope that they are fortunate enough to find a cure and regain the moral health that they were given when entering this life.

15. Nature

Nature and the natural world also have an association with poverty and wealth. A love and appreciation of nature enriches us immeasurably, and yet, we may also impoverish ourselves by neglecting and destroying nature.

We have known this since ancient times, but still, in our modern global culture of greed, we destroy natural habitats, one after another. Our callous and short sighted actions also drive species into extinction and yet, we need this diversity of species to maintain a balance within the natural world, upon which, we, ourselves depend. Again. we have appreciated this since ancient times, but we allow our insatiable greed to overrule any such appreciation or considerations of care for our natural world. Of course, as part of The Great Deception, we organise a multitude of government quangos and committees whose task is to look into this very problem. Decades pass by and no decisive conclusions are ever reached. What treachery and duplicity continues to fund these 'pretend' organisations while, in Britain for example, we continue to build everywhere, destroying natural habitats and environments even on land which was previously protected and designated as Green Belt. This gross hypocrisy is a facet of the greed culture which places the making of money above all else, even our own longer term survival. In governmental and commercial centres, those who love nature are condemned as freaks or troublemakers whenever they try to protect a threatened habitat.

From the global perspective, our duplicity in this respect is quite worrying. We rattle on for ages about global warming, using it as an excuse to raise taxes or the cost of energy to the consumer, but the real danger to humanity is habitat destruction. Every time we destroy another natural habitat, whether on land or at sea, and no matter how small, we are destroying another part of the broader tapestry of life. Already, that tapestry is beginning to look like a patchwork quilt. At some juncture, we shall reach the point of no return where the damage we have wreaked upon the natural world, plus the sheer weight of human population, will render it impossible to repair the damage. Sceptics will scoff and claim that we shall always find an answer with technology. But technology, as ingenious as it is, will never replace the wonderful and beautiful complexity of nature and the complex web of interactions and dependencies which it maintains. Our technology is infantile in the extreme compared with nature.

In all our destructiveness, we believe that we are somehow creating wealth. Certainly, we are making money. Money for the property developers and builders. Money for the organisations who sell off the natural resources, such as timber, or who use the land to grow genetic crops. Money for the corrupt politicians who overturn protection orders or otherwise intervene on behalf of the money makers. But we do not create wealth. We create poverty. Furthermore, with each ill-considered selfish bit of destruction, we reduce the long term potential for the survival of the human race. This is not scare mongering, but simple arithmetic. Our current actions and attitudes are simply not sustainable into the longer term. By staying on this trajectory we are, in fact, betraying future generations. This does not sound like wealth.

What is true in the general sense is also true at a personal level. To ignore nature is to lead an incomplete life. Not to understand nature is to exist in ignorance. There is nothing more important than nature and the natural world. We are an integral part of this world and it is an inseparable part of us. For those who take the trouble to look closely; to understand evolution and the workings of nature, to appreciate the remarkable beauty in all of nature's exquisite designs, to develop a love of animals and their world, they will discover a wealth beyond any riches manufactured or imagined by mankind. To love nature is to love life, at its deepest level.

Those who scoff and stand by happily as we destroy the natural world around us are living in the poorest of poverty. The man who has never felt the soft carpet of the moors under his feet, has never drunk from a mountain stream, has never

Nature

wandered through the wilderness, has never touched a tree or marvelled at the beauty of a leaf, is poor indeed. The man who goes further and actually destroys natural habitats for profit, is poor beyond measure.

Returning again to ancient Egypt, it is curious how, even in the old and middle kingdoms, they appreciated the natural world and the distinct characters of the animals with whom they shared it. Little wonder then that animals played such a large part in their deities. They also understood respect for the land and how not to over-farm it. And, of course, they respected the annual rising and falling of the great river, measuring its progress meticulously every year. They knew how to coexist with the natural world around them. The Australian aborigines also had, and maintain to this day, a respect for the natural world. Native Americans were able to coexist with nature and adapted their own movements to the rhythms of the natural world. The great art of historic Europe was often inspired by nature, whether in image, music or the written word.

We simply cannot separate ourselves from the

natural world. We were born and have developed within it. We have admired and wondered at it for many thousands of years. Our understanding of it now is perhaps greater, from a scientific perspective, than it has ever been. How can we now betray it in such a horrible way? That is like murdering our own mother. Behaving like this is to revel in poverty. It is time that we understood and celebrated the wealth of nature. Not for its entertainment value, as is so often the case these days, but for itself. The wonder of creation is the ultimate wealth. There is none higher.

16. Conclusion

This book has examined the concepts of poverty and wealth and attempted to place them into a better, more positive perspective. Furthermore, it has outlined how we often mistake one for the other, not realising the longer term difficulties to which such a misunderstanding leads. Of course, some might look upon this as the ramblings of an old man who is living in a by-gone age. Actually, nothing could be further from the truth as the distinction is more pertinent today than it has ever been.

Our misguided view of wealth is distorted by the universal culture of greed that has engulfed the modern world during the past few decades. One might argue that things have always been that way, but this is not true. Even immediately post war in the late 1940s and 1950s, people had an entirely different attitude towards such things. There was a much stronger sense of community and sharing within the community. People talked to each other; not just peers, but those from entirely different backgrounds. Adults spoke to children and children to adults. People had time for one another. Consumer goods offered real value with their cost reflecting the cost of manufacture in a way that never happens today. Education, health care and local administration all seemed to function so much easier, and produced better results.

What on Earth has gone wrong? Why have we thrown so much away for so little in return? Citizens the world over are fed a yarn about technology, entertainment and celebrity as part of The Great Deception, while really important factors are ridiculed or ignored altogether. In addition, we seemed to have dumbed down education to simply an artificial means to an end. We believe that if someone understands IT and current technology, then this is all the education they need in order to have a successful career. Our interpretation of success having become so grossly distorted as to mean simply the acquisition of material wealth.

Conclusion

Success as a human being no longer enters the equation. It is all about making money. And those who make money, often by dishonest means which bring distress to others, are held up as icons of our modern society. We confer celebrity status upon all the wrong people, not for their value as human beings or what they do for others, but for how much money they make, or because they are part of popular music or entertainment culture. Those who are of real value to society are studiously ignored.

This is a common factor of what we like to call 'wealthy' societies. In fact, in many ways, they are impoverished societies. Often, they are societies who deny their own history for reasons of political correctness. Societies who rob their citizens through dishonest, but legal, practices as exploited by the giant corporations and banks. Societies wherein the individual is unimportant, unless he or she has cash in their hand. Societies who believe it acceptable for teenagers to leave school illiterate. Societies who allow the elderly to die, unattended in hospital corridors, while the directors of the same hospitals pay themselves obscenely large salaries. Societies where banks and financial organisations have successfully lobbied government to enable them to legally cheat their customers. Societies where nothing seems to have any inherent quality, no matter how high the cost. Societies where art has become a meaningless parody of real artistic merit. In short, we seem to have gone backwards during the last half a century.

What hope is there of changing this around and returning to a world of proper values? Well, there is always hope, but hope often needs a helping hand. The first step is to acknowledge that things have gone awry and that our sense of values has become distorted. If we deny this reality, then there truly is no hope. If, on the other hand, we acknowledge that things need to change, then we can sit down and apply some intelligent thought as to how to bring about this change.

If we are to create a truly wealthy society where all the wonders of the world, including the more positive human achievement, are understood and celebrated by all, regardless of their position, then we must start with education. Not just formal education as taught as part of the curriculum in schools, but education in every sense. At home, through the media and in everything that we create.

Conclusion

It should all be aimed at explanation and education of all that is good, both in modern society and within the wonderfully rich heritage of art, literature, music and architecture that we have inherited. Especially important is education about our wonderful planet. Its geological mechanisms and the evolution of life on Earth. Only by understanding these things may one appreciate the beauty and wonder of the natural world, as well as its importance to our own survival.

This education also needs to take place in the home. But how can this be if parents themselves are ignorant and have no interest, except in the material world? It may be a process that needs to take place over a number of generations. However, we have to start somewhere, and those first steps may certainly be made within our educational systems. And all of our educational systems, from kindergarten through secondary schools and on to universities. Indeed, universities in many countries are in disarray, caught between trying to act as an incubator for commercial activities and a long term repository for career academics by their tens of thousands. This was not the original concept and we need to return to first principles in this respect.

And the education should never stop. Even within industry, commerce and government, individuals should be constantly learning, at least, learning that which is good and positive. It is perhaps in government where this new wave of education could have the most dramatic effect. Educating government ministers to create intelligent policies which care for and protect their citizens and their countries would really start to create a better world. These policies should include a sensible level of control and accountability with regard to large corporations and industry in general. They should always be in support of citizens and, for every step taken, the question should be asked; 'how is this enriching or improving the lives of our citizens?' If an answer cannot be found, then the step should not be taken.

We cannot change the past, nor the consequences of past mistakes. But we can strive to create a better future. A future based upon intelligent policies, social justice and education. That is something that we should feel honour bound to do for future generations. However, just look around you at what is happening today. The unbridled culture of greed, supported by government, is trampling over

Conclusion

everything that is pure and good. It is destroying our world in return for short term material gain, with no thought for the future. Its very hypocrisy has created The Great Deception whereupon all true values are trashed and replaced with nonsensical assertions about technology, entertainment and celebrity. How can youngsters grow up with any sense of proportion when exposed, day by day, to such nonsense? Surely, it is time we came to our senses and rekindled the flame of decency, honour and justice in order that it may burn brightly and light the way to a new tomorrow.

Dismiss this book if you will, as the ramblings of an old man with outdated opinions. However, to do so would be a mistake. Let it instead spark a new strain of thought within your own consciousness. A strain of thought which might, in time, create a new thread within the great tapestry of life to help restore it to where it should be. Start in your own back yard and witness the positive influence that you might bring to bear, helping others to also rekindle their powers of understanding, observation and reason. The very powers which The Great Deception seeks to extinguish.

Of Poverty and Wealth

Finally, think about those concepts of poverty and wealth and what they really mean, both with respect to your own life and from the broader perspective. We often confuse one with the other. Yet, throughout history, there have been those that have understood the distinction. Currently, they may be few and far between, but they are there. Why not come and join them and help to make the world a better place?

17. Epilogue

It may seem to the reader, initially, that the focus of this work has been upon the exposure of greed and the pursuance of wealth for its own sake. This is true to a point, but it is really about the damage that such attitudes wreak upon our global culture. Indeed, upon civilisation itself. Being able to determine that which is real, spiritual wealth and that artificial wealth based purely upon material possessions and the acquisition of money, is a first step towards repairing this damage.

Due to illness, this book is not as comprehensive in scope as the author would have liked. However, it has hopefully made its point and stirred within the reader some more serious consideration of these topics. For those who understand this, perhaps they might continue the work by researching and producing their own dissertations upon the subject. Perhaps they might use this book as a discussion vehicle, in order to solicit views from others, having scoured these pages. Perhaps they might even start their own movement in calling for a reassessment of social values.

The human species has, over the millennia, achieved so much which is good and positive. Its efforts have resulted in what we have, with some justification, termed 'civilisation'. We have created wonderful works of art, built astonishing structures and developed scientific thought. What a tragedy it would be if all this were allowed to deteriorate and bring destruction to our world. At first, such comments might sound like scare mongering. But think again. Our very existence is actually quite fragile. Our narrow minded, obscene preoccupation with money and material wealth will seem trivial indeed if and when the very survival of humanity becomes in question. And yet, our attitudes and actions are drawing this question ever closer. It is time to start asking awkward questions. It is time to re-examine concepts such as poverty and wealth and place them within a correct and intelligent context.

Epilogue

Read this book. And then read it again. Use it to inform and inspire deeper discussion upon the subject. For there is no subject more important as we progress into the twenty first century.

Notes

Of Poverty and Wealth

Made in the USA
Charleston, SC
31 January 2017